I0191124

LEGION

Legion

Glory Unveiled

Mike VanOuse

Copyright © 2019 Mike VanOuse

All rights reserved

ISBN: 978-1-7342702-0-4

Legion
Glory Unveiled

Table of Contents

Text

This treatise is an examination of the biblical account of the "Demoniac of Gadara," which occurs in three gospels. Before we parse the elements, let's first peruse the text:

Matthew 8:
28   *And when he was come to the other side into the country of the Gergesenes, there met him two possessed with devils, coming out of the tombs, exceeding fierce, so that no man might pass by that way.*
29   *And, behold, they cried out, saying, What have we to do with thee, Jesus, thou Son of God? art thou come hither to torment us before the time?*
30   *And there was a good way off from them an herd of many swine feeding.*
31   *So the devils besought him, saying, If thou cast us out, suffer us to go away into the herd of swine.*
32   *And he said unto them, Go. And when they were come out, they went into the herd of swine: and, behold, the whole herd of swine ran violently down a steep place into the sea, and perished in the waters.*
33   *And they that kept them fled, and went their ways into the city, and told every thing, and what was befallen to the possessed of the devils.*
34   *And, behold, the whole city came out to meet Jesus: and when they saw him, they besought [him] that he would depart out of their coasts.*

Next:

Mark 5:
1   *And they came over unto the other side of the sea, into the country of the Gadarenes.*
2   *And when he was come out of the ship, immediately there met him out of the tombs a man with an unclean spirit,*
3   *Who had [his] dwelling among the tombs; and no man could bind him, no, not with chains:*
4   *Because that he had been often bound with fetters and chains, and the chains had been plucked asunder by him, and the fetters broken in pieces: neither could any [man] tame him.*
5   *And always, night and day, he was in the mountains, and in the tombs, crying, and cutting himself with stones.*

6   *But when he saw Jesus afar off, he ran and worshipped him,*

7   *And cried with a loud voice, and said, What have I to do with thee, Jesus, [thou] Son of the most high God? I adjure thee by God, that thou torment me not.*

8   *For he said unto him, Come out of the man, [thou] unclean spirit.*

9   *And he asked him, What [is] thy name? And he answered, saying, My name [is] Legion: for we are many.*

10   *And he besought him much that he would not send them away out of the country.*

11   *Now there was there nigh unto the mountains a great herd of swine feeding. {5:12} And all the devils besought him, saying, Send us into the swine, that we may enter into them.*

13   *And forthwith Jesus gave them leave. And the unclean spirits went out, and entered into the swine: and the herd ran violently down a steep place into the sea, (they were about two thousand;) and were choked in the sea.*

14   *And they that fed the swine fled, and told [it] in the city, and in the country. And they went out to see what it was that was done.*

15   *And they come to Jesus, and see him that was possessed with the devil, and had the legion, sitting, and clothed, and in his right mind: and they were afraid.*

16   *And they that saw [it] told them how it befell to him that was possessed with the devil, and [also] concerning the swine.*

17   *And they began to pray him to depart out of their coasts.*

18   *And when he was come into the ship, he that had been possessed with the devil prayed him that he might be with him.*

19   *Howbeit Jesus suffered him not, but saith unto him, Go home to thy friends, and tell them how great things the Lord hath done for thee, and hath had compassion on thee.*

20   *And he departed, and began to publish in Decapolis how great things Jesus had done for him: and all [men] did marvel.*

And finally:

Luke 8:

26   *And they arrived at the country of the Gadarenes, which is over against Galilee.*

27   *And when he went forth to land, there met him out of the city a certain man, which had devils long time, and ware no clothes, neither abode in [any] house, but in the tombs.*

28   *When he saw Jesus, he cried out, and fell down before him, and with a loud voice said, What have I to do with thee, Jesus, [thou] Son of God most high? I beseech thee, torment me not.*

29   *(For he had commanded the unclean spirit to come out of the man. For oftentimes it had caught him: and he was kept bound with chains and in fetters; and he brake the bands, and was driven of the devil into the wilderness.)*

30   *And Jesus asked him, saying, What is thy name? And he said, Legion: because many devils were entered into him.*

31   *And they besought him that he would not command them to go out into the deep.*

32   *And there was there an herd of many swine feeding on the mountain: and they besought him that he would suffer them to enter into them. And he suffered them.*

33   *Then went the devils out of the man, and entered into the swine: and the herd ran violently down a steep place into the lake, and were choked.*

34   *When they that fed [them] saw what was done, they fled, and went and told [it] in the city and in the country.*

35   *Then they went out to see what was done; and came to Jesus, and found the man, out of whom the devils were departed, sitting at the feet of Jesus, clothed, and in his right mind: and they were afraid.*

36   *They also which saw [it] told them by what means he that was possessed of the devils was healed.*

37   *Then the whole multitude of the country of the Gadarenes round about besought him to depart from them; for they were taken with great fear: and he went up into the ship, and returned back again.*

38   *Now the man out of whom the devils were departed besought him that he might be with him: but Jesus sent him away, saying,*

39   *Return to thine own house, and shew how great things God hath done unto thee. And he went his way, and published throughout the whole city how great things Jesus had done unto him.*

Elements

Matthew says there were two demoniacs, Mark and Luke both say that there was one. Matthew says they were in the country of Gergesenes, while Mark and Luke say it was the country of Gadarenes. Neither of these differences change the outcome: that Jesus confronted a demoniac(s) whom the local authorities couldn't tame, delivered him from satanic dominion, and all that ensued.

Gergesenes and Gadara are not two distinct countries: they were two cities near each other in a cluster of towns East of the Sea of Galilee, referred to in scripture as "Decapolis," translated: "the ten cities."

Before becoming a disciple and Apostle of Christ, Matthew was a tax collector whom Jesus recruited on the fly. Jesus, passing by his work station, said, "Follow Me," and Matthew left all to follow Him[1]. Matthew was the only eyewitness to the account of the three gospel writers.

Mark was a protégé to the Apostle Peter. It's assumed that the Gospel of Mark was dictated to him by Peter, who also witnessed the account (Mark may or may not have been there).

Luke was a traveling companion of the Apostle Paul who didn't witness the account. Luke, being a physician by profession was the most highly-educated of the gospel writers. He compiled his gospel from interviews with those directly involved, to include Mary, the mother of Jesus. And he did his footwork: his gospel is considered one of the most detailed and accurate historic accounts of the period.

The four Gospels – Matthew, Mark, Luke and John – tell the same story from four different perspectives. It's as if a traffic accident happened in the middle of an intersection, and the four gospels are the accounts of four witnesses who were standing on separate corners of the intersection. It stands to reason that they would each see different things.

But it's not as though they were journalists who submitted scoops to their editors the same day it happened. Scholars estimate that the Gospel of Matthew was written somewhere between 50 and 70 AD. Jesus was crucified circa 33 AD. That puts a minimum gap of 17 years between the event and its record.

---

1   Matthew 9:9

Likewise the authorship of Mark is pegged at about 60 AD, and Luke at 50-80 AD. So while time had elapsed from the event to its recording and peripheral details vary, the pertinent elements agree.

Nevertheless, it's a confounding story. Why would Jesus accede and grant the petition of demons? Aren't they enemies of God and intrinsically evil? Why didn't He show such compassion toward the poor local townsfolk who raised pork for a living? Surely He knew what the outcome would be : He's God – He knows everything.

How was God glorified in showing up uninvited, making a mess, destroying the local economy, and being urged by the community to leave post haste? To top it off, when the beneficiary of His handiwork asked to accompany Him, He denied him permission. Rejection hurts. How is that merciful?

The object of this treatise is to answer all of those questions and reveal the understated glory buried in the midst of this account.

Details

Jesus had a tendency to say and do things that caused most of the audience to say, "What the heck was that all about?" walking away befuddled. For example, when the disciples of the John the Baptist pointed out that they and the disciples of Pharisees would regularly fast (abstain from eating) and that Jesus' disciples didn't, part of His response was that nobody patches an old garment with new cloth, or puts new wine in old wine-skins.[2]

While that may be true, the common observer would think, "What has that got to do with anything?"

It was an oblique way of saying, "I didn't come to add a new take on the Jewish religion: I'm launching a whole new program that doesn't fit in with your routine. There's a new Sheriff in town."

Sometimes the object of the obscurity was that He was only addressing a target audience. When He came to Jerusalem and cast the money-changers out of the temple – overturning their tables, scattering their wares and driving them out with a scourge – He remained to teach the masses.

The temple officials showed-up in force, demanding, "Tell us, by what authority do you do these things?" He answered (paraphrase), "John the Baptist: was He from God, or of man? Answer me, and I'll answer you." They said, "We can't answer." He said, "Then neither will I answer you."[3]

Then He went on to tell a story about a vineyard owner who sent messengers to the husbandmen, that they should send him his cut of the profits from the harvest. But the husbandmen beat and killed the messengers and the owner's son. So the vineyard owner would destroy the husbandmen[4].

That story probably meant absolutely nothing to the general audience gathered before Him. But the temple officials, who were scholars of the scriptures, knew exactly what He was saying[5]. It was an allusion to a prophesy in Isaiah where the vineyard represented the nation of Israel[6], and the husbandmen were the leaders – the very officials Jesus was addressing.

---

2   Mark 2:18-22
3   Matthew 21:23-27
4   Matthew 21:33-46
5   Matthew 21:45
6   Isaiah 5:7

They showed up after He cast out the peddlers and thieves to say, "We've come to remove you!" His answer, encrypted for their private consumption was, "Au contraire: I've come to remove You." Again, "There's a new Sheriff in town."

Such is the case with the demoniac of Gadara. The target audience of His activity there wasn't the swine herders. Nor was it the Apostles. It was the thrones and dominions, powers and principalities[7]: invisible rulers of spiritual wickedness in high places[8] who had established a stronghold in that geographic location. He was letting them know that the party was over, brandishing His new Sheriff's badge.

Let's take a look at that geographic location.

---

7   Colossians 1:16
8   Ephesians 6:12

Location

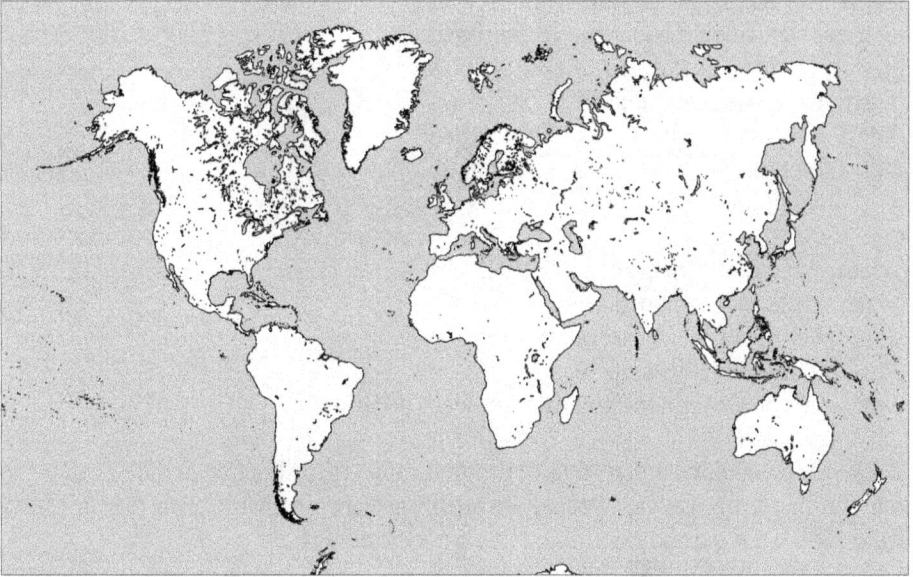

Figure 1

You are here ▲

To the center-right of Figure 1 is where all the events of the Bible take place: Israel and the surrounding areas.

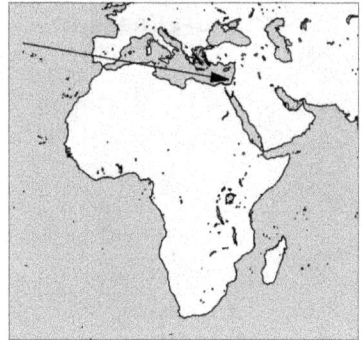

Israel

Figure 3

Figure 2

In the North-East corner of Israel is the Sea of Galilee, or the Sea of Tiberias.

Matthew's account begins: *"And when he was come to the other side into the country of the Gergesenes..."*

9

He was coming from the fishing village of Capernaum to the "other side" of the Sea of Galilee.

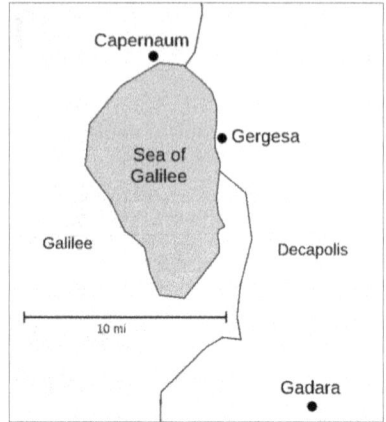

Figure 4

Galilee, to the West, or left of the Sea of Galilee, was Jewish territory. To the East, or, "other side" of the Sea of Galilee was pagan territory: Heathenville. The Jews didn't like the heathen, and the heathen didn't like them. They didn't associate with one another.

When the ship embarked from Capernaum, Jesus took a nap in the back of the ship. Then a storm arose on the sea, so tempestuous that the ship was taking on water and the fishermen thought they were doomed.

When they wakened Jesus to tell Him that they were about to perish, He said to the wind and the waves, "Peace! Be still!" and the sea went calm (Mt 8:23-27, Mk 4:39). That was a new thing. New Sheriff: new rules.

Figure 5

Most read these two stories – the calming of the sea and the demoniac of Gadara – as isolated episodes. But coupling them together as one makes sense when viewed in a broader context to other passages, and extra-biblical references to the region.

In Matthew 16, Jesus and His posse departed by ship from Magdala (from whence cometh Mary Magdalene), and crossed back over to the heathen side of the Sea of Galilee.

> v:13 *When Jesus came into the coasts of Caesarea Philippi, he asked his disciples, saying, Whom do men say that I the Son of man am?*

What is a coast? As you can see by Figure 5, Caesarea Philippi is pushing 30 miles to the North, and it doesn't have coasts: it has borders. Coming to the coasts would be landing the ship near the same area where the swine had previously run violently down the hill, choking in the sea. It may well have been the same spot. Maybe not.

When Simon answered the Lord's question, saying that He was the Christ, Jesus renamed him:

> v:18 *And I say also unto thee, That thou art Peter, and upon this rock I will build my church; and the gates of hell shall not prevail against it.*

Many take comfort in believing that this means the church can withstand any attack from hell. But gates don't attack anything: they're defensive edifices. What Jesus was saying is that when the church attacks the gates of hell, those gates will not be able to withstand the onslaught.

Whether they were on the ship, on the shore or on the way, it was in reference to Caesarea Philippi when He said that.

Caesarea Philippi has a unique terrain feature: a cave with a spring of water that serves as tributary to the Jordan called, "the Grotto of Pan." You can visit it or look it up on line today. It bears that name because the locals of Jesus' day believed that the pagan-deity, "Pan," of the Roman pantheon lived in the cave.

Figure 6. "The Grotto of Pan" Caesarea Philippi (Image adapted from http://3.bp.blogspot.com/)

Further, the Jewish Historian Josephus records that attempts were made to sound for the depth of the spring, and the bottom couldn't be found[9].

According to Greek (Hellenistic) customs that predate Roman conquest, the world of the dead – "Hades" – lies deep underground: "the netherworld." The locals of Caesarea Philippi believed that this cave was the "bottomless pit:" the portal to the netherworld.

Another way to say that is, "The Gates of Hell."

---

9   Josephus, Flavius "The Wars of the Jews," Book 1, Chapter 21, Paragraph 3

Events

Caesarea Philippi lies in the valley of Lebanon off the South-West side of Mount Hermon, facing the Sea of Galilee. Not only is it home to the Grotto of Pan, but Mount Hermon is littered with the ruins of pagan idols and temples. The entire region was a hotbed of occult practices.

According to 1 Enoch, Mount Hermon is the location where angelic beings called,"watchers" descended and took an oath to rebel against God[10] (Although not canonized as inspired text, 1 Enoch is cited by both Peter[11] and Jude[12], lending credence to the text. The watchers are mentioned in Daniel[13]).

The Bible doesn't refer to the pagan gods as make-believe fairy-tale creatures as Western civilization does. It refers to them as devils, much like the demons Jesus cast into the herd of swine. You may believe that they're imaginary fantasy creatures, but Jesus didn't. Neither did the Apostle Paul[14] or any of the other writers of the New Testament[15]. Fantasies don't drown pigs.

The devil wants you to believe that he and his minions don't exist. This grants them freedom to operate: to steal, kill and destroy without opposition[16]. Bullies don't seek opposition; they seek victims.

Some devils are more powerful than others. There are thrones, dominions, powers, principalities and several tiers of satanic authority. The honchos can manipulate natural forces. In the Book of Job, Satan caused fire to fall from the sky and destroy Job's flocks and servants[17]. He caused a great wind to destroy the house where Job's children were feasting, killing them all[18].

And it was a great wind that met the ship coming from Capernaum carrying Jesus as he approached the gates of hell[19]. The devils know who He is[20]. They saw Him coming. They said, "Uh-oh: We're in trouble now!"

---

10   1 Enoch 6:4
11   2 Peter 2:4
12   Jude 1:6
13   Daniel 4:13, 17
14   1 Timothy 4:1
15   James 2:19
16   John 10:10
17   Job 1:16
18   Job 1:19
19   Mark 4:37
20   Mark 3:11, Acts 19:15 et al.

(None of this dialog is recorded in scripture, but the circumstantial evidence suggests it. It's what scholars call a "theological inference," as opposed to employing poetic, literary or artistic license).

Then one of them said, "Hey look – He's asleep! Now's our chance," and they cooked-up a tempest to repel the vessel. But tempests aren't a big deal to God. It wouldn't be surprising to find out that Jesus took His little nap just to bait them into taking that swing so He could glorify His Father by demonstrating His supremacy over nature. Either way, that was the result.

Or do you suppose that sudden storm took Him by surprise? He's God, not a meteorologist.

Since the storm-front artillery failed to stop the invasion, the principalities switched to "Plan B:" "Send in the Infantry: the legion in the demoniac with the strength to break chains! They're so fierce that no man can pass!"

When Jesus hit the beachhead, the demoniac ran screaming at Him, challenging His presence. Then Jesus broke his spiritual chains and set him free. Problem solved. "Next!"

The demons, realizing they'd been abandoned by their overlords, suddenly became docile and begged Jesus not to cast them into the deep.

(They were standing on the edge of a sea, so a cursory reading of "the deep," implies that they didn't want to end up in the water {which they did}. But the word translated into English as "the deep," in the original Greek manuscripts, is more accurately rendered, "the abyss," or Tartarus: the spiritual dungeon of torment alluded to in 2 Peter 2:4 and Jude 1:6.)

When Jesus granted their prayer, the demons entered the pigs and the pigs went berserk, stampeding to a watery grave like thirsty lemmings. Then the towns-folk asked Jesus to skedaddle. So He did.

Jesus answers prayer: He granted the pleas of the demons and the locals; but not of the former demoniac who asked if he could tag along. To that He said, "No, go home and tell everyone what God has done for you."

Jesus didn't kill the pigs; they committed suicide of their own volition. He didn't abandon the townspeople without a livelihood; they asked Him to depart of their own volition. He was well able to reimburse their loss: He'd fed thousands of people with a few loaves and fishes[21].

---

21   Matthew 14:13-21, Mark 6:32-44, Luke 9:10-17, John 6:1-15

But instead of praying for restitution, they prayed for Him to depart. Just like the sudden storm on the sea, He knew all these things would transpire as a result of His visit, yet He went ahead and did it anyway.

Why? Answering the prayers of demons and heathen but not of a redeemed soul is counter-intuitive to the nature of a God of order, who is supposed to be harsh to the wicked, merciful to the good, benevolent and graceful. How does such a story of bedlam, mayhem and destruction glorify God?

Unveiled

Remember who the target audience was: the invisible evil rulers of darkness.

In a seemingly unrelated passage, after having cast out a spirit, Jesus explained:

> Matthew 12:
> 28   *But if I cast out devils by the Spirit of God, then the kingdom of God is come unto you.*
> 29   *Or else how can one enter into a strong man's house, and spoil his goods, except he first bind the strong man? and then he will spoil his house.*

The East side of the Sea of Galilee represented, geographically, the kingdom of Satan: the gates of hell. When Jesus arrived, it was the kingdom of God invading the kingdom of Satan. After having demonstrated His supremacy over the storm on the sea, He demonstrated His supremacy over the gods that the local inhabitants worshiped by liberating their most notorious prisoner.

Demons consider the people they inhabit to be their houses[22].

He entered into the strong man's house, overpowered him, and spoiled his goods. The pigs were quite possibly being raised for ritual sacrifice to be slaughtered for the devils. Jesus set them loose and spoiled their ritual.

What about the upset locals? They were gripped with fear. Why? Perhaps they believed the demon-gods they worshiped were going to be angry. They thought the favor of the devils was necessary to bless the fertility of their crops and herds in order for their economy to flourish. Now their means of appeasing the devils had been dunked away and there might be repercussions.

They didn't stay upset long though. Mark's account appears in chapter 5 of his gospel. In chapter 6, Jesus spooked His posse by walking on water (another new Sheriff thing). After calming them down and getting into the ship, they landed again on the heathen side of the Sea of Galilee:

> Mark 6:
> 53   *And when they had passed over, they came into the land of Gennesaret, and drew to the shore.*

---

22   Matthew 12:43-45

> 54   *And when they were come out of the ship, straightway they knew him,*
> 55   *And ran through that whole region round about, and began to carry about in beds those that were sick, where they heard he was.*
> 56   *And whithersoever he entered, into villages, or cities, or country, they laid the sick in the streets, and besought him that they might touch if it were but the border of his garment: and as many as touched him were made whole.*

Weird: They didn't ask Him to leave this time – rather, they ran to Him. Why?

Remember Jesus refusing the demoniac's prayer? Let's recapitulate Mark's account:

> Mark 5:
> 18   *And when he was come into the ship, he that had been possessed with the devil prayed him that he might be with him.*
> 19   *Howbeit Jesus suffered him not, but saith unto him, Go home to thy friends, and tell them how great things the Lord hath done for thee, and hath had compassion on thee.*
> 20   *And he departed, and began to publish in Decapolis how great things Jesus had done for him: and all [men] did marvel.*

After demonstrating His supremacy over nature in the tempest, and supremacy over the devil's kingdom by storming his beach, plundering his house, and spoiling his goods; Jesus dispatched the beneficiary of His handiwork on a mission causing all men (in ten cities) to marvel, turning their hearts to God.

Then Jesus returned, healing their diseases and setting more of the devil's prisoners free, destroying the works of the devil[23], accentuating His preeminence over the forces of darkness in ALL CAPS. The invisible powers and principalities understood it full well – and it stung.

And that's how such a confusing story of mayhem and destruction brings glory to God, our merciful Savior. It was a humiliation of His adversary. Jesus didn't cross the sea to make a mess: He Crossed to clean the mess up. It wasn't an invasion; it was a liberation.

He whom the Son sets free is free indeed. That's what He does.

Glory to God.

---

23   1 John 3:8

www.ingramcontent.com/pod-product-compliance
Lightning Source LLC
Chambersburg PA
CBHW071942020426
42331CB00010B/2981